What I Understand Now

It's the love I couldn't see healing the distance between and parents and adult children

BY

DR. JANET OLIVARES

What I Understand Now

Published by Glorybound Publishing, Camp Verde, AZ
SAN 256-4564
Published in the United States of America
1st Edition
ISBN 978-1-60789-384-4 1-60789-384-3
Copyright data is available on file.
Olivares, Janet, 1955-
What I Understand Now /Janet Olivares
Includes biographical reference.
1. Self-Help 2. Family Counseling

I. Title

www.raphaccc.org
www.gloryboundpublishing.com

Scripture quotations are from the Holy Bible.

Understand this book is not intended as a substitute for consultation with a licensed practitioner. This book is intended for educational and inspirational purposes only. It is not a substitute for professional mental health or legal advice. Please consult with your own physician or health care specialist regarding the suggestions and/or recommendations in this book. The use of this book implies your acceptance of this disclaimer. Thank you.

For counseling services or speaking engagements:
Rapha Christian Counseling Center
info@raphaccc.org

What I Understand Now

It's the love I couldn't see healing the distance between and parents and adult children

BY DR. JANET OLIVARES

Glorybound Publishing
Camp Verde, Arizona USA
in the year 2026

Dedication

To the parent who felt the distance
and didn't understand why.

To the one who kept showing up
even when it felt like it didn't matter.

To the parent who heard,
"I don't want to come"
and felt something break inside—
but stayed anyway.

This book is for you.

Your child may not have the words
to explain what they are feeling.
What comes out may sound like rejection…

But it is not always a lack of love.

There is more happening
beneath what you can see.

Do not give up.

Even when it feels quiet.
Even when it feels one-sided.

Because sometimes…
the love you think is gone
is still there—
just waiting to be understood.

Introduction

There are moments that stay with us.

Not because they were loud…
but because they were confusing.

A child standing at the door.
A parent waiting for an answer.
A quiet "I don't want to go."

And in that moment—
everything feels clear.

It feels like rejection.

But what if it wasn't?

What if that moment…
the one that stayed with you…
was never meant to push you away?

Children do not always have the words
to explain what they are feeling.

They don't always understand
why something feels too big inside them.

So they say what they can.
They react the only way they know how.

And sometimes…
what comes out sounds like rejection.

But it isn’t rejection.

It’s confusion.
It’s being overwhelmed.
It’s a child trying to make sense of two worlds
they didn’t choose to live between.

And on the other side of that moment—
is a parent.

A parent who loves deeply.
A parent who is trying.
A parent who hears those words
and feels something shift inside.

Not just hurt…
but distance.

And slowly, without meaning to,
a story begins to form.

“They don’t want me.”
“They are pulling away.”
“Maybe I’ve already lost them.”

But what if that story isn’t true?

This book exists for that space.

The space between what was said…
and what was actually meant.

The space between what was felt…
and what was understood.

Through the eyes of a child
and thc rcflcction of the adult they become,
you will begin to see something different.

Not perfectly.
Not all at once.

But clearly enough
to release what was never meant to stay heavy.

This is not a book about blame.

It is not about choosing sides.

It is not about proving who was right or wrong.

It is about understanding.

It is about seeing what was hidden
beneath words that were never fully explained.

It is about recognizing that love
was often present—
even when it did not feel like it.

Because sometimes…

What feels like rejection
may actually love
that didn't yet know how to stay steady.

And when we begin to understand that—
something changes.

The story softens.
The weight lifts.
The distance no longer feels permanent.

And from that place…

Healing becomes possible.

This is where your understanding begins.

Why This Book Matters to Parents

There is something many parents carry quietly.

Not just the moments that were hard…
but the questions that never fully settled.

Did I do enough?
Did I handle it right?
Did I lose them somewhere along the way?

And the one question that often stays the longest:

Did it matter?

This book is not written to go back and change what happened.

It is written to help you understand what your child may not have been able to say at the time.

Because what sounded like rejection…
was not always rejection.

What looked like distance…
was not always a loss of love.

And what felt like the end of connection…
may have simply been a moment that needed more time to be understood.

If you stayed—
even imperfectly,
even unsure,
even when it felt like it wasn't enough—

this book is for you.

Because sometimes…

What a child understands later
changes everything.

What I Understand Now

Program Overview

What I Understand Now is a faith-based emotional healing and restoration program designed to help parents, adult children, co-parents, and families better understand the emotional impact of relational distance, misunderstanding, unresolved hurt, and emotional disconnection within family systems.

This program focuses on helping individuals recognize how fear, confusion, emotional overwhelm, inconsistency, and unspoken pain often become misinterpreted as rejection. Through reflective storytelling, emotional insight, practical repair strategies, and Biblical principles, participants are guided toward greater understanding, compassion, communication, emotional safety, and restoration.

Rather than focusing on blame, this program helps participants:

- Understand emotional responses within family relationships
- Identify hidden pain beneath conflict and withdrawal
- Learn the importance of emotional safety and repair
- Recognize how misunderstanding impacts parent-child relationships
- Develop healthier communication and relational stability
- Build emotional awareness and accountability
- Encourage healing, forgiveness, and restoration

This program may be used:

- Individually
- In counseling sessions
- In reunification work
- In family restoration programs
- In parenting/co-parenting support
- In church small groups
- In adult healing and recovery settings

The goal of this program is not perfection.
The goal is understanding, emotional growth, steadiness, repair, and restoration through truth, compassion, and Biblical principles.

What I Understand Now

Learning Objectives

By the completion of this program, participants will be able to:

Emotional Understanding

- Identify how children and parents often misinterpret emotional experiences within family relationships.
- Recognize how confusion, fear, emotional overwhelm, and inconsistency can be mistaken for rejection.
- Understand the long-term emotional impact of unresolved family conflict and emotional disconnection.

Communication & Emotional Safety

- Identify the role emotional safety plays in healthy family relationships.
- Understand how tone, consistency, emotional regulation, and repair influence connection and trust.
- Develop greater awareness of how emotional reactions affect children and family systems.

Personal Reflection & Healing

- Identify false beliefs carried from childhood related to worth, rejection, blame, or responsibility.
- Recognize how unresolved emotional wounds may continue affecting adult relationships and communication patterns.
- Develop insight into personal emotional triggers and relational responses.

Repair & Restoration

- Learn practical repair strategies to restore emotional connection after conflict or misunderstanding.
- Demonstrate healthier approaches to emotional regulation, listening, and relational repair.
- Understand the importance of steadiness, consistency, and emotional presence in rebuilding trust.

Faith & Growth

- Apply Biblical principles of grace, restoration, forgiveness, peace, and compassion within family relationships.
- Recognize how faith, truth, and understanding support emotional healing and restoration.
- Develop healthier relational patterns that promote long-term emotional stability and connection.

Table of Contents

What I Understand Now

PART 1 — Understanding

CHAPTER 1

What I Thought Was Rejection

I didn't understand it then.
I didn't have the words to explain what I was feeling.
But what I understand now is something very different.

Through the Eyes of the Child I Was

I didn't understand it then.

I didn't have the words
to explain what I was feeling,
so I created meaning
from what I could see.

And what I saw…
felt like rejection.

But what I understand now
is something very different.

I am not ten anymore.

I want to say I'm an adult with a voice…
but I still have a long way to grow.

I am still learning how to understand parents.
Still learning how to understand what happened.

But there are things from when I was younger
that stayed with me longer than I realized.

Not loud things.
Not always obvious things.

Just quiet conclusions I made
when I didn't understand what was happening around me.

I didn't say them out loud.

But I believed them.

I believed:

They stopped trying.
They let me go.
They didn't fight for me.

And the one that stayed the longest…

Maybe I just wasn't worth it.

No one sat me down and told me that.

No one used those exact words.

But when things changed…
when visits felt different…
when conversations got shorter…
when distance slowly grew…

That's what it felt like.

And feelings—when they stay long enough—
start to feel like truth.

What That Looked Like in Real Life

It looked like small moments.

Moments most people wouldn't notice.

Sitting in the car
not wanting to get out.

Not because I didn't care…

but because I didn't know
what I was walking into.

Walking into a house
and trying to read the room
before saying anything.

Listening carefully to tone.

Trying to figure out:

Is this a good moment?
Should I stay quiet?
Should I say something?

Sometimes feeling relief
when it was time to leave.

And not understanding why.

Sometimes missing someone
even when I had just seen them.

Nothing about it felt clear.

But all of it felt important.

What I Remember Most

I remember watching.

Watching tone.
Watching faces.
Watching what wasn't said.

I remember wondering:

Did I do something wrong?
Should I be different?
Should I say less?

I remember trying to fix something
I didn't understand.

Trying to make things feel normal again.

Sometimes I tried harder.
Sometimes I pulled back.

Sometimes I said things like,
"I don't want to go."

But what I meant was something deeper.

I meant:

"I don't understand what's happening."
"I don't feel steady."

"I don't know where I belong right now."

But I didn't have those words yet.

So what came out…

sounded like rejection.

What I Wish Someone Had Told Me Then

I wish someone had said:

"You're not the problem."
"You're allowed to feel this way."
"You don't have to figure this out alone."

I wish someone had said:

"This isn't about your worth."

Because that is what I questioned the most.

What I Didn't Understand Then

I thought my voice pushed people away.

I thought my emotions made things worse.

I thought my confusion created distance.

I thought if I had just been easier…
quieter…
less emotional…

Maybe

things would have stayed the same.

Maybe they would have stayed closer.

Maybe they would have fought harder for me.

What I Understand Now

I was not rejected.

I was loved
by people
who did not always know
how to stay steady
when things became hard.

I was loved by a parent
who felt overwhelmed
and didn't know how to fix what was breaking.

I was loved by a parent
who felt like they were losing
and didn't know how to reach me
without making things worse.

The Moment I See Clearly Now

I had a voice.

But my voice didn't always sound like truth.

To them…
it sounded like distance.

And their silence…

felt like rejection to me.

The Misunderstanding That Happens in Families

This is where many families quietly break.

Not in loud moments.
Not in one big decision.

But in misunderstanding.

Children feel:

"They stopped choosing me."

Parents feel:

"They don't want me anymore."

And somewhere in between…

love gets buried
under what neither side knows how to explain.

A Truth I Wish I Knew Sooner

Parents don't always pull away
because love is missing.

Sometimes they pull away

because they feel like they are already losing you.

Sometimes they pull away
because they don't know what to do next.

Sometimes they pull away
because their own fear
becomes louder than their strength.

What I thought was rejection…

was not always rejection.

What Was Really There

There may have been:

Fear
Self-doubt
Guilt
Emotional exhaustion
Not knowing what to say
Not knowing how to fix it

Not a lack of love.

What Changed for Me

Everything began to shift
when I asked a different question.

Not:

"Did they love me enough?"

But:

"What were they going through
that I couldn't see?"

That question didn't erase the pain.

But it gave it context.

And context…

creates space for understanding.

Faith and Restoration

There is something else I understand now.

What felt broken
was not beyond repair.

What felt lost
was not gone forever.

Because God does something
we often forget in the middle of pain:

He restores.

What was divided
can be brought back together.

What was misunderstood
can be made clear.

What felt like rejection
can be revealed as love
that simply didn't know how to stay strong.

But restoration does not happen automatically.

We must be willing to ask for it.
To see differently.
To open the door again.

Closing Thought

What I thought was rejection
was not always rejection.

Sometimes…

it was love
struggling to find its way back.

Closing Line

Children don't just remember what happened.

They remember
what they believed it meant.

PART 1 — Understanding

CHAPTER 2

When My Voice Sounded Like Rejection

I didn't understand it then.
I didn't have the words to explain what I was feeling.
But what I understand now is something very different.

Through the Eyes of the Child I Was

At the time,
my words felt honest.

They felt like the only way
to explain what was happening inside me.

But I didn't understand
how those words sounded
to the people who loved me.

What I meant
and what they heard
were not the same.

And now…
I can finally see the difference.

I remember saying things
I didn't fully understand.

"I don't want to go."
"I don't like it there."
"I'm staying here."

The words came out quickly.

Sometimes with emotion.
Sometimes with frustration.
Sometimes with tears.

At the time,
they felt honest.

They felt like the only way
I could explain what was happening inside me.

But I didn't realize then…

how those words sounded
to the adults listening.

What That Looked Like in Real Life

It looked like standing near the door
when it was time to leave…

and feeling something tightening inside me.

It looked like:

Moving slower on purpose
Hoping no one noticed
Hoping maybe plans would change

It looked like:

Saying "I don't want to go"
but not knowing how to explain why

It looked like:

Getting quiet in the car
or talking too much
just to avoid what I was feeling

It looked like:

Trying to hold it together
so no one would get upset

And sometimes…

it looked like tears
that didn't make sense
even to me.

What I Meant

I didn't mean:

"I don't love you."
"I don't want you."
"I am choosing someone else."

I wasn't making a decision
about one parent over the other.

I was trying to explain a feeling
I didn't have language for yet.

I meant:

"I feel overwhelmed."
"I don't know what to expect."
"I feel different in each place."
"I don't feel steady."

I meant:

"Something inside me doesn't feel okay…
and I don't know how to fix it."

What I Wish Someone Had Heard

I wish someone had heard past my words.

I wish someone had said:

"You don't have to explain it perfectly."
"I can see something feels hard."
"You're allowed to feel this way."

Because I wasn't trying to reject anyone.

I was trying to be understood.

What It Sounded Like to Them

But that's not what they heard.

They heard:

"They don't want to be with me."
"They are choosing the other parent."
"I'm losing my child."

And when someone feels like they are losing
something they love…

they react.

Sometimes they try harder.
Sometimes they push.
Sometimes they question.

And sometimes…

they pull away.

The Moment Things Shift

There is a moment most families don't notice.

It doesn't feel big at the time.

But it changes everything.

It's the moment when:

A child speaks from confusion…
and a parent hears rejection.

From that moment forward…

The child feels misunderstood.
The parent feels hurt.

And both begin protecting themselves
without realizing it.

What Repair Could Have Looked Like

There was something that moment needed…
that I didn't understand at the time.

Not correction.
Not pressure.
Not explanation.

A pause.

A return.

Repair.

Instead of reacting…
the moment could have slowed down.

It could have sounded like:

"I think there's something more you're trying to say."
"You don't have to explain it perfectly."
"I'm here. We can figure this out."

Because what I needed
was not to be fixed.

I needed to be understood
in the middle of what I couldn't explain.

Repair doesn't solve everything.

But it keeps the connection
from breaking in the moment it feels the most fragile.

What It Felt Like for Me

I remember feeling like my words made things worse.

Like every time I tried to explain…
something got heavier instead of clearer.

I remember thinking:

Maybe I shouldn't say anything.
Maybe I should just go along with it.
Maybe my feelings are the problem.

So sometimes I stop talking.

And sometimes…

my silence said even more
than my words ever did.

The Hidden Fear I Carried

There was something else I felt
that I didn't know how to say.

"I don't want to hurt anyone."

I didn't want one parent to feel rejected.

I didn't want the other to feel like I was choosing sides.

So I held things in.

And when I did speak…

it came out wrong.

What I didn’t understand then… was that my feelings were real, even if my words weren’t clear.

Not because it wasn’t real.

But because I didn’t have the words yet.

What Was Really Happening Inside Me

I was adjusting.

To two homes.
Two sets of expectations.
Two emotional environments.

I was trying to figure out:

Where do I relax?
Where do I watch?
Where do I speak?
Where do I stay quiet?

That takes energy.

More than most adults realize.

And when you are carrying that much…

even small things
can feel big.

What I Understand Now

My voice wasn’t rejecting.

It was expression
without clarity.

What sounded like rejection… was really a child trying to be understood.

It was emotion
without language.

It was confusion
trying to be heard.

What Happens When Fear Gets Involved

When a child says,
"I don't want to go" …

What parents heard as rejection… was often a child asking for safety.

it doesn't land as neutral.

It lands in a place
that already feels vulnerable.

Parents often feel:

Rejected
Replaced
Unwanted
Afraid

And fear does something powerful.

It makes people react
instead of understanding.

What Could Have Changed Everything

There needed to be a pause.

Not a reaction.
Not a defense.

A pause.

A moment to ask:

"What is my child feeling
that they don't yet know how to say?"

What That Might Have Looked Like

If someone had slowed the moment down…

Instead of:

"Why don't you want to come?"
"Are you choosing them over me?"

It could have been:

"Help me understand what feels hard."

"You're allowed to feel that way."
"I'm here."

And in that kind of space…

I might have found better words.

What This Means Now

If you were the child who said:

"I don't want to go"
"I don't want to be there"

You need to hear this clearly:

That did not mean
you didn't love your parents.

Love was still there… it just didn't come out in a way anyone could understand yet.

It meant something inside you
needed understanding.

And If You Are the Parent

If you are the parent who heard those words…

You need to hear this too:

That was not rejection.

That was your child
trying to make sense of something
they didn't understand.

Faith and Restoration

Misunderstanding is one of the quietest ways
families become divided.

Not because love is missing.

But because words are misheard
and feelings are misinterpreted.

The enemy works in that space.

In confusion.

In assumption.
In silence.

But God restores truth.

He brings clarity
where there was confusion.

He helps us hear
what was really being said…

not just what it sounded like in the moment.

Closing Thought

Children don't always say what they mean.

But they always mean
what they feel.

Closing Line

Sometimes what sounds like rejection
is really a child asking
to feel safe again.

CHAPTER 3

When Parents Felt Rejected Too

I didn't understand it then.
I didn't have the words to explain what I was feeling.
But what I understand now is something very different.

Through the Eyes of the Adult I Am Now

I only saw what I was feeling.

I didn't see
what it felt like on the other side.

I didn't understand
that while I was trying to make sense of my world…
someone else was trying not to lose me.

I couldn't see it then.

But I can see it now.

There is something I didn't understand as a child.

I thought I was the only one hurting.

I thought I was the only onc confused.

I thought I was the only one trying
to hold things together
without knowing how.

But I see it differently now.

What I thought was distance… was often pain I didn't know my parents were carrying.

I wasn't the only one carrying something heavy.

My parents were too.

What That Looked Like in Real Life

It didn't look obvious.

It wasn't always loud.

It wasn't always spoken.

It looked like:

A pause before responding
A change in tone I couldn't quite explain
Moments that felt distant
even when we were in the same room

It looked like:

Shorter conversations
Less eye contact
A feeling that something had shifted
but no one said why

It looked like:

Trying again…
and then trying less

At the time…

I didn't understand what I was seeing.

I only felt it.

What I Thought Then

When things became distant…
when communication changed…
when effort felt different…

I believed something simple:

They stopped trying.
They gave up.
They chose something else.

And I didn't question it.

Because from where I stood…

that's what it looked like.

What I See Now

They didn't stop caring.

They didn't stop loving.

They didn't stop wanting a relationship with me.

They started doubting.

Doubting themselves.
Doubting what to say.
Doubting how to fix it.
Doubting if they were already losing me.

And doubt…

can be louder than love
when someone doesn't know what to do next.

What Rejection Feels Like to a Parent

I didn't understand this before.

But I do now.

When a parent hears:

"I don't want to come."
"I don't want to be there."

They don't hear confusion.

They hear loss.

They hear

"I'm not chosen."
"I'm being replaced."
"I'm no longer wanted."

And that kind of pain…

doesn't always lead to clarity.

When a Parent Feels Rejected — What Helps

There is a moment
that feels heavier than most.

The moment a parent hears:

"I don't want to come."
"I don't want to be there."

And something inside them shifts.

It feels personal.
It feels final.
It feels like loss.

And in that moment…
everything in a parent wants to protect.

To pull back.
To stop trying.
To avoid feeling that again.

But that is the moment
repair is needed the most.

Repair sounds like:

"That was hard to hear… but I'm still here."
"I don't understand yet… but I want to."
"You don't have to push me away to be honest."

Repair is not ignoring the pain.

It is choosing connection
even while feeling it.

What That Might Have Felt Like for Them

I didn't see it then…

but I can imagine it now.

Trying to reach your child
and feeling like it's not working.

Wanting to say the right thing
but being afraid of saying the wrong one.

Wondering:

"Am I making this worse?"
"Should I push or give space?"
"What if they don't want me anymore?"

And sitting with those questions…

without knowing what to do next.

The Quiet Pullback

Parents don't always leave loudly.

Sometimes they step back quietly.

They stop pushing.
They stop asking.
They stop trying as hard.

Not because love disappeared…

But because they don't know how to reach without making things worse.

What I Didn't See as a Child

I didn't see:

The hesitation before they spoke
The fear behind their silence
The emotional weight they were carrying
The exhaustion of trying
without knowing if it mattered

I didn't see the moments they were trying to hold it together inside.

I only saw the distance.

When Both Sides Feel Rejected

This is where families quietly begin to break.

Thc child feels:

"They stopped choosing me."

The parent feels:

"They don't want me."

And both begin to step back.

Not out of a lack of love…

But out of fear of losing more.

What Fear Does

Fear doesn't always look like panic.

Sometimes it looks like:

Silence
Distance
Less effort
Avoiding hard conversations
Not reaching out

Fear says:

"Don't make it worse."
"Don't push too hard."
"Don't risk more rejection."

And without realizing it…

love becomes quieter.

What I Understand Now

My parents didn't reject me.

They felt rejected.

And instead of knowing how to move closer…

they moved carefully.

And sometimes…

carefully looks like distance.

What This Changes

When the story changes…

Everything begins to shift.

Instead of:

"They stopped loving me."

The truth becomes:

"They didn't know how to reach me
without risking losing me more."

What I Wish I Could Say to Them Now

If I could go back…

I would say:

"You didn't lose me."
"I didn't stop loving you."
"I just didn't know how to say what I needed."

And maybe…

that would have changed something.

What Parents Need to Hear

If you are a parent reading this…

Your child's words
may have touched something deeper in you.

A fear of losing them.
A fear of not being enough.
A fear of being replaced.

And if you pulled back…

it may not have been because you didn't love them.

It may have been because you didn't know
how to move forward without making things worse.

What Children Need to Understand

If you are the child—now older—reading this…

Your parent's distance
may not have been their decision.

It may have been their uncertainty.

It may have been their fear.

It may have been their way of protecting
what little connection they felt they still had.

Faith and Restoration

The enemy works quietly in moments like this.

Not through loud conflict…

but through assumption.

Through silence.
Through misinterpretation.
Through unspoken pain.

But God works in truth.

He reveals what was hidden.
He softens what was hardened.
He restores what was misunderstood.

And sometimes…

He allows us to see later
what we could not understand then.

What Healing Looks Like

Healing doesn't begin with blame.

It begins with understanding.

Because understanding
creates space for compassion.

And compassion…

opens the door for restoration.

Closing Thought

They didn't always know how to reach you.

But that doesn't mean
they didn't want to.

Closing Line

Sometimes parents don't step back
because they don't care…

Sometimes they step back
because they care deeply
and don't know how to move forward.

What This Means Now

If you are the parent:
What you felt was real.
That moment may have felt like loss…
like something was slipping away.

But your child was not leaving you.
They were trying to understand something
they didn't have words for yet.

If you are the child—now grown:
Your parent's distance
may not have been a lack of love.
It may have been uncertainty…
fear…
not knowing how to reach you without making it worse.

If you are both:
You may have been standing in the same moment—
feeling the same fear—
and interpreting it in completely different ways.

And sometimes…
what felt like rejection on both sides
was actually love
that didn't know how to move closer.

PART 1 — Understanding

CHAPTER 4

When Love Was There — But Strength Was Missing

I didn't understand it then.
I didn't have the words to explain what I was feeling.
But what I understand now is something very different.

Through the Eyes of the Adult I Am Now

I thought love
should have looked stronger.

I thought it would have shown up
more clearly…
more consistently…
more steady.

When it didn't,
I questioned if it was there at all.

But what I didn't understand then…
was that love can be present
even when people feel overwhelmed.

Now,
I see what I couldn't see before

There is a truth I didn't understand as a child.

It would have changed everything
if I had known it then.

Love and strength
are not always the same thing.

And sometimes…

love is present
even when strength is not.

What That Looked Like in Real Life

It didn't look like someone who didn't care.

It looked like moments that didn't stay steady.

It looked like:

Good days
followed by hard ones

Calm conversations
followed by quick reactions

Moments of connection
followed by distance

It looked like:

Not knowing which version of the day
I was going to walk into

It looked like:

Trying to relax…
but staying aware

Trying to be myself…
but adjusting just in case

And even though love was there…

it didn't always feel consistent.

What I Thought Then

When things felt inconsistent…
when effort came and went…
when connection didn't feel steady…

I believed something simple.

If they loved me, they would have shown up.
If they cared, they would have done more.
If I had mattered, they would have been stronger.

That made sense to me then.

Because as a child…

love and action felt like the same thing.

What I Understand Now

Love was there.

But strength was not always available.

Strength to stay calm
Strength to handle conflict
Strength to face rejection
Strength to keep trying
when it felt like nothing was working

Strength to lead
when emotions were overwhelming

What Strength Really Means

Strength isn't loud.

It's not force.

It's not control.

Strength looks like

Staying calm when emotions rise
Listening without reacting
Holding space without shutting down
Continuing to show up
even when it feels difficult

And that kind of strength…

is learned.

Not everyone has it
when they need it most.

What Strength Looks Like in Real Moments

Strength is not about being perfect.

It is not always knowing what to say.

It is not never getting it wrong.

Strength looks like something quieter.

It looks like it is repaired.

It sounds like:

"That didn't come out right."
"I got overwhelmed."
"Let's try that again."

Strength is the ability
to come back
after the moment didn't go well.

Because children don't need perfection.

They need to know
that when something breaks…

it will be repaired.

Consistency builds safety.

But repair…
rebuilds it when it breaks.

What Weakness Really Looks Like

As a child, I thought weakness meant:

They don't care.
They are choosing something else.

But weakness often looks very different.

It looks like:

Shutting down
Avoiding conflict
Getting overwhelmed quickly
Not knowing what to say
Not knowing how to respond
Pulling back instead of leaning in

It looks like:

Trying…

but not knowing how to stay steady

Weaknesses are not the absence of love.

It is the absence of capacity
in difficult moments.

The Truth Many Children Never Hear

Adults struggle too.

Not because they are bad.

Not because they don't love their children.

But because:

They were never taught how to regulate emotions
They were never shown steady parenting
They are carrying their own pain
They are overwhelmed and unsure

And when pressure rises…

their ability to stay steady
falls.

What I Didn't See Then

I didn't see:

The internal battles they were fighting
The emotions they were trying to manage
The fear of doing the wrong thing
The weight they were carrying

I only saw what didn't happen.

I didn't see what they were trying
to hold together inside.

What Happens When Strength Is Missing

When strength is missing…

love becomes inconsistent.

And inconsistency creates confusion.

Children begin to wonder:

Can I trust this?
Will this last?
Should I protect myself?

Not because love isn't there…

but because it doesn't feel steady.

The Conclusion Children Often Make

When love feels inconsistent…

children don't think:

"They are struggling."

They think:

"I am not enough."

And that is where the misunderstanding takes root.

What Needs to Be Separated

This is the truth that brings healing:

Love
and ability
are not the same thing.

A parent can:

Love deeply
and still struggle to show it well

Care deeply
and still respond poorly

Want connection
and still do not know how to maintain it

What This Changes

If you ever believed:

"They didn't love me enough"

You may need to consider something different:

They may not have had the strength

to show love in a steady way.

What I Wish I Understood Then

I wish I had known:

It wasn't about my worth.

It wasn't about me not being enough.

It was about something they
had not yet learned how to do.

What This Means for Parents

If you are a parent reading this…

You may have loved your child deeply…

But struggled to:

Stay calm
Stay consistent
Stay emotionally present

That does not erase your love.

But it may explain
what your child experienced.

Where Growth Begins

Growth does not begin in shame.

It begins with awareness.

Because once we understand:

"I loved… but I wasn't steady"

We can begin to grow into:

"I love… and I am learning to stay steady"

Faith and Restoration

There is hope here.

Because what we lacked…

God can build.

Where we were weak…
He strengthens.

Where we were overwhelmed…
He steadies.

Where we didn't know what to do…
He teaches.

Scripture reminds us:

"My grace is sufficient for you, for My power is made perfect in weakness."
— 2 Corinthians 12:9

Weakness is not the end of the story.

It is where restoration begins.

What Healing Looks Like

Healing begins when we stop asking:

"Did they love me enough?"

And start asking:

"What were they capable of in that moment?"

Because with that answer…

Everything often changes.

Closing Thought

Love may have been there the whole time…

Even when strength was not.

Closing Line

A lack of strength
does not mean a lack of love…

It means
there is still room to grow.

What I Understand Now

PART 2 — Internal Healing

CHAPTER 5

When I Thought I Was the Reason

I didn't understand it then.
I didn't have the words to explain what I was feeling.
But what I understand now is something very different.

When I Thought I Was the Reason

Through the Eyes of the Child I Was

I carried questions
that felt like answers.

Questions about my worth.
Questions about what I had done wrong.

And over time,
those questions
started to feel like truth.

I didn't know how to separate
what I felt
from what was real.

But I understand that now.

There was something I carried
for a long time…

Something I didn't talk about.

Not because I didn't feel it…

but because I thought

it was mine to hold.

I thought I was the reason
things changed.

I thought I was the reason
things got harder.

I thought I was the reason
things fell apart.

No one sat me down and said:

“This is your fault.”

But when you are a child…

You don’t need to be told.

You fill in the blanks yourself.

What That Looked Like in Real Life

It looked like replaying moments
over and over in my mind.

Thinking:

“Maybe I shouldn’t have said that.”
“Maybe I should have just stayed quiet.”
“Maybe I made it worse.”

It looked like:

Watching how people reacted to me
and trying to adjust

Trying to be:

Easier
Quieter
Less emotional

Or sometimes…

trying harder to be noticed
hoping that would fix something

It looked like:

Feeling responsible
for things I didn't understand

The Questions I Asked Myself

I remember asking myself:

Did I say something wrong?
Did I make it harder?
Did I choose wrong?
Was I too emotional?
Was I too much?

Or maybe…

not enough?

The Quiet Weight Children Carry

Children are always trying
to make sense of their world.

And when something doesn't make sense…

they look for a reason.

The easiest place to look
is inward.

"If something changed…
maybe it was me."

Why Children Blame Themselves

Because it gives them
a sense of control.

If I caused this…
maybe I can fix it.

If I change…
maybe everything will go back
to the way it was.

So children try.

They become quieter.
Kinder.
More careful.

Or sometimes…

they become louder.
Angrier.
More reactive.

But underneath it all
is the same question:

"What do I need to do
to make this better?"

What I Didn't Understand Then

I didn't understand
that I was trying to fix
something that was never mine to carry.

I didn't understand
that adult decisions,
adult emotions,
and adult struggles…

do not belong to a child.

How It Followed Me

What I believed then
didn't stay in childhood.

It followed me.

Into how I saw myself.
Into how I handled relationships.
Into how I responded to conflict.

It showed up as:

Overthinking
Trying to keep everyone happy
Avoiding hard conversations
Feeling responsible for everything

It showed up as:

Fear of getting it wrong
Fear of losing people
Fear of not being enough

All connected to something I believed
when I was younger.

What I Understand Now

I was not the reason.

I was a child
trying to understand a situation
that was bigger than me.

I was responding
to changes I didn't create.

I was feeling
what I didn't know how to explain.

What Needs to Be Said Clearly

Children are not responsible
for adult relationships.

Not for:

Conflict
Distance
Separation
Emotional struggles
Decisions made by adults

Even when children have strong emotions…

Even when they say things like:

"I don't want to go"
"I'm staying here"

That is not the cause.

That is the response.

The Burden of False Responsibility

When a child believes:

"I caused this"

They begin to carry something heavy.

Guilt

Shame
Confusion
Self-doubt

And those feelings don't stay in childhood.

They follow into adulthood.

They show up in ways
that don't always make sense.

What I Wish Someone Had Told Me

I wish someone had said:

"This is not your fault."
"You didn't cause this."
"You don't have to fix this."

I wish someone had taken
that weight off my shoulders
before I carried it so long.

What Needs to Be Released

This is where healing begins.

Not by pretending it didn't hurt

But by correcting
what wasn't true.

You were not the reason.

You were in the middle
of something
you didn't create.

What This Means for You Now

If you have ever thought:

"If I had been better…"
"If I had said something different…"
"If I had just stayed quiet…"

Pause here.

Take that weight

off your shoulders.

It was never yours to carry.

What This Means for Parents

If you are a parent reading this…

Your child may be carrying things
you never meant for them to carry.

And unless it is said clearly…

they may continue carrying it
into adulthood.

Sometimes healing begins
with simple words:

"This was never your fault."

Faith and Restoration

God never placed adult responsibility
on a child.

He does not ask children
to carry what belongs to adults.

Scripture reminds us:

"Cast all your anxiety on Him because He cares for you."
— 1 Peter 5:7

That includes the weight
you picked up as a child.

God restores
not only what was broken…

but what was misunderstood.

What Healing Looks Like

Healing looks like this:

"I was not the reason."

And then slowly…

"I don't need to carry that anymore."

Closing Thought

You were never too much.

You were never the problem.

You were a child
trying to understand something
that was never yours to fix.

Closing Line

Children don’t cause the breaking.

They feel it.

CHAPTER 6

Why Love Didn't Always Feel Safe

I didn't understand it then.
I didn't have the words to explain what I was feeling.
But what I understand now is something very different.

Through the Eyes of the Child I Was

I didn't question love.

I questioned how it felt.

I didn't understand
why something that was supposed to feel safe…
sometimes didn't.

So I adjusted.
I guarded.
I learned to read the room.

But now,
I understand where that feeling came from.

There is something I didn't understand when I was younger.

I thought love
was supposed to feel safc all the time.

I thought if someone loved me…

I would feel calm.
I would feel secure.
I would feel steady.

But that's not what I always felt.

And I didn't know what to do with that.

What That Looked Like in Real Life

It looked like walking into a room
and feeling something shift inside me…

before anything was even said.

It looked like:

Listening carefully to tone
Trying to read expressions
Watching for signs
that something might change

It looked like:

Not knowing if it was a good moment
or a hard one

It looked like:

Feeling okay one minute
and unsure the next

It looked like:

Trying to relax…
but not fully letting myself

Not because I was unsafe

but because I didn't feel steady.

What I Felt But Couldn't Explain

I didn't have the words:

"I don't feel emotionally safe."

So I said:

"I don't want to go."
"I don't like it there."

But what I meant was:

"I don't know what I'm walking into."
"I don't know how things are going to feel."
"I don't know how to relax here."

What Safety Feels Like to a Child

Safety is not just physical.

It is emotional.

It feels like:

Calm voices
Predictable responses
Being allowed to be yourself
Not having to guess what mood someone is in

It feels like:

You can breathe
You can speak
You can be quiet

Without worrying
something will suddenly change.

What Made Things Feel Unsteady

It wasn't always big things.

Sometimes it was small moments
that happened often enough
to matter.

It could have been:

Raised voices
Quick reactions
Unpredictable emotions
Tension in the room
Feeling like I had to be careful

Even subtle shifts…

when repeated over time…

become something a child feels deeply.

What I Thought Then

I didn't think:

"This environment feels emotionally inconsistent."

I thought:

"Something is wrong with me."
"Why can't I just be okay here?"

So I tried to adjust.

What I felt wasn't wrong… it just didn't have understanding around it yet.

I tried to be easier.
Quieter.
More careful.

But the feeling didn't fully go away.

What Happens Inside a Child

When emotional safety feels uncertain…

The body responds

It becomes:

Alert
Watchful
Careful

Even if the child
doesn't understand why.

They begin to:

Scan the room
Watch tone and expression
Adjust their behavior
Become more aware
than they should have to be

And over time…

they may begin to pull back.

Not from love

but from the feeling.

What I Understand Now

Love was there.

But safety didn't always feel steady.

And when safety feels uncertain… love can be hard to recognize.

And children respond more
to what they feel
than what they are told.

What Parents Often Don't Realize

Parents may say:

"But I love you."
"I would never hurt you."

And that may be completely true.

But love and emotional safety
are not always experienced
the same way.

What Needs to Be Understood

Children don't pull away
from love.

They pull away
from what doesn't feel safe.

And sometimes… that gets mistaken for rejection.

How Safety Is Rebuilt

Safety is not built
by getting everything right.

It is built
by what happens after things go wrong.

Because moments will happen.

Voices will rise.
Emotions will take over.
Things will not come out the way they should.

But safety is restored
in the return.

Repair sounds like:

"That got loud. I'm sorry."
"You didn't deserve that tone."
"I want to do that differently."

It sounds like:

"I'm still here."
"We're okay."
"We can try again."

Children don't need perfect environments.

They need environments
where repair happens.

Because safety is not found
in the absence of mistakes.

It is found
in what follows them.

What This Changes

Instead of asking:

"Why don't they want to be with me?"

The question becomes:

"What does it feel like
to be with me?"

That question changes everything.

What I Wish Someone Had Helped Me Understand

I wish someone had said:

"It's okay if something feels hard."
"You're not wrong for feeling this."
"We can figure this out together."

Because I thought
the problem was me.

Not the environment
I was trying to adjust to.

What This Means for You

If you were the child who felt this…

You were not wrong.

You were responding
to what your body and emotions
were experiencing.

What This Means for Parents

If you are a parent reading this…

This is not about blame

It is about awareness.

Because once you understand this…

you can begin to change it.

What Safety Can Become

Safety can be built.

Not perfectly.

But consistently.

Through:

Calm responses
Predictability
Listening without reacting
Allowing space for feelings

It doesn't require perfection.

It requires steadiness.

Faith and Restoration

God is not only a God of love.

He is a God of peace

Scripture tells us:

"For God is not a God of confusion but of peace."
— 1 Corinthians 14:33

Where there was confusion…

He brings clarity.

Where there was tension…

He brings peace.

Where safety felt uncertain…

He restores what was missing.

What Healing Looks Like

Healing begins when we understand:

"I loved them…
but I didn't always feel safe."

And then we allow that truth
to guide change…

not blame.

Closing Thought

Love may have always been there.

But safety is what allows love
to be fully felt.

Closing Line

Children stay where they feel safe…

not just where they are loved.

CHAPTER 7

When Things Break… and Repair Guide

I didn't understand it then.
I didn't have the words to explain what I was feeling.
But what I understand now is something very different.

Through the Eyes of the Adult I Am Now

At the time,
a break felt final.

A moment felt like the whole story.

I didn't understand
that things could be repaired…
that connection could return…
that not everything was permanent.

I only knew
what it felt like in that moment.

Now,
I understand what repair really means.

**There is something I didn't understand as a child.

I thought relationships broke
in big moments.

I thought something had to happen
that couldn't be undone.

Something loud.
Something final.
Something that meant…
it was over.

But that's not what I see now.

Relationships don't usually break
in one moment.

They break
in the moments after.

What I Thought Then

When something felt wrong…
when voices changed…
when distance showed up…

I thought:

"This is what it is now."

I thought the moment defined everything.

I thought:
If something went wrong…
it stayed wrong.

So I adjusted.

I got quieter.
More careful.
More aware.

Not because I stopped loving…
but because I didn't know
things could be repaired.

What I Understand Now

Moments don't define relationships.

What happens after the moment does.

There is something that changes everything.

Something most families were never taught.

Something simple…
but powerful.

Repair.

What Repair Really Is

Repair is not perfect.

It is not getting everything right.

It is not avoiding mistakes.

Repair is what happens
after something goes wrong.

It is the return.

It is the moment someone says:

"That didn't feel right."
"Let's slow this down."
"I'm still here."

Repair is connection
coming back
after it was interrupted.

What That Looked Like in Real Life

As a child…

When something felt off
there was no return.

No one came back
to explain it.

No one slowed the moment down.

No one said:

"That got hard… let's try again."

So the moment stayed
the way it felt.

And over time…

Those moments added up.

Not because they were big.

But because they were never repaired.

What Happens When Repair Is Missing

When repair is missing…

Children don't think:

"That was just a hard moment."

They think:

"This is what it is."

"This is what I can expect."

"This is what I need to prepare for."

And slowly…

They begin to adjust.

They become:
More aware
More careful
More quiet

Not because love is gone…

But because safety feels uncertain.

What Repair Would Have Changed

It wouldn't have required perfection.

It wouldn't have required the right words every time.

It would have required something much simpler.

Coming back.

Saying:

"That didn't come out right."
"I got overwhelmed."
"You didn't deserve that tone."
"Let's try again."

That is what changes everything.

What Repair Feels Like to a Child

Repair feels like:

Relief

Like something settled

that didn't stay broken.

It feels like:

"I'm still safe here."
"This isn't permanent."
"They didn't leave me in that moment."

Repair tells a child:

"Even when things go wrong…
we come back."

What I Understand Now

It wasn't the hard moments
that stayed with me.

It was the ones
that were never repaired.

Because without repair…

The moment becomes the meaning.

What This Means for Parents

If you are a parent reading this…

You do not need to be perfect.

You will have moments:
Where you react
Where you feel overwhelmed
Where things don't come out right

That is not what breaks connection.

What matters is what happens next.

Repair sounds like:

"I'm sorry for how I handled that."
"I want to understand you."
"I'm here."

It is not weakness.

It is strength.

What This Means for Children (Now Adults)

If you were the child in those moments…

You may still be carrying what was never repaired.

Not because it was intentional.

But because it was never addressed.

And that can feel like:

Distance
Confusion
Unanswered questions

But understanding something now
changes what you carry.

It allows you to see:

That moment
was not the whole story.

When Both Sides Don't Know How to Repair

Sometimes…

Neither side knew what to do.

The child didn't have the words.

The parent didn't have the tools.

And the moment stayed unfinished.

Not because love was missing…

But because repair was missing.

What Repair Looks Like Now

Repair doesn't have to happen perfectly.

It just has to happen.

It can sound like:

"That was hard earlier."
"I've been thinking about that moment."
"I don't want to leave it like that."

It can be simple.

It can be quiet.

But it matters.

What Repair Does Over Time

One repair
may not change everything.

But consistent repair…

Changes how a relationship feels.

It builds:

Trust
Safety
Stability

It teaches:

"We don't stay broken."

Faith and Restoration

God does not leave us
in broken moments.

He restores.

He returns.

He meets us again.

Scripture reminds us:

"The Lord is close to the brokenhearted
and saves those who are crushed in spirit."
— Psalm 34:18

God does not expect perfection.

He offers restoration.

And through Him…

we learn to do the same.

What Healing Looks Like

Healing does not come
from avoiding hard moments.

It comes from learning
how to return from them.

From saying:

"We are not finished here."

Closing Thought

It was never the mistake
that broke the connection.

It was the absence of repair.

Closing Line

Relationships don't break
because something went wrong…

They break
when no one comes back.

What This Means Now

If you are the parent:
You do not have to get every moment right.
What matters most
is that you come back.

Not with perfection—
but with presence.

If you are the child—now grown:
The moments that hurt
may not have been the end of the story.

What matters now
is whether connection can be rebuilt—
not exactly as it was…
but in a way that is honest and real.

If you are both:
Repair does not erase what happened.
But it changes what happens next.

And sometimes…
the strength of a relationship
is not measured by what was never broken—
but by the willingness
to come back after it was.

REPAIR GUIDE

How to Repair, When Something Breaks… This Is How We Come Back

Repairing something is about coming back after something went wrong.

Moments will happen.
Voices may raise.
Feelings may get hurt.

What matters most is what happens next.

Step 1: Pause

Do not rush to fix it with more words.

Take a breath.
Let your body calm down.

Repair begins when we are steady not reactive.

Step 2: Come Back Gently

Approach with calm, not control.

Sit (near), not above.
Keep your voice soft.

This is not a time for lectures.
This is a time for connection.

Step 3: Acknowledge What Happened

Name it simply.

"That felt hard."

"I didn't handle that well."

"I see that upset you."

No blaming.
No defending.

Just honesty.

Step 4: Take Responsibility (Even in Small Ways)

Even if it wasn't all your fault own your part.

"I should have slowed down."

"I wish I would have listened better."

This builds safety.

Step 5: Reassure the Relationship

Children (and even adults) need to know:

The relationship is still safe.

"I love you."

"We are okay."

"I'm not going anywhere."

Repairs restore security.

Step 6: Invite, Don't Force

Give space for response.

"Do you want to tell me how that felt?"

"I'm here if you want to talk."

If they are not ready respect that.

Connection cannot be forced.

Step 7: Return to Normal Together

Repair is complete when calm returns.

Sit together.
Do something simple.
Let the moment settle.

Not everything needs to be discussed deeply.

Sometimes healing is quiet.

Remember

It was never the moment that caused the deepest hurt…
It was when no one came back.

Truth to Hold Onto

You do not need to get it right every time.
You only need to come back.

Because coming back
is what teaches a child…

"I am safe."
"I am loved."
"We can get through hard things together."

If you want next, I can…

PART 2 — Internal Healing

CHAPTER 8

Why I Came Back

I didn't understand it then.
I didn't have the words to explain what I was feeling.
But what I understand now is something very different.

Through the Eyes of the Adult I Am Now

There were moments
where distance felt easier.

Where pulling away
felt safer than staying close.

I didn't have the words
to explain why I came back…
or what I was looking for.

But something in me
kept returning.

Now,
I understand why.

For a long time…

I didn't know how to explain it.

Why I pulled away.
Why I felt distant.
Why some relationships felt easier than others.

And eventually…

why I came back.

It wasn't one moment.

It wasn't one conversation.

It wasn't something someone said perfectly.

It was something quieter than that.

Something I felt
before I could explain it.

What That Looked Like in Real Life

It looked like I was noticing small things.

A calmer response
when I expected frustration.

A conversation
that didn't turn into pressure

A moment where I felt heard
instead of corrected

It looked like:

Not having to explain everything perfectly
Not feeling like I had to defend myself
Not feeling like I had to choose

It looked like:

Being able to sit in the same space
without tension building.

And slowly…

Something inside me started to relax.

What Didn't Bring Me Back

It wasn't pressure.

It wasn't guilt.

It wasn't being told
what I "should" do.

It wasn't reminders of:

"What I've done for you"

"This is your family"
"You need to come"

Those things didn't draw me closer.

If anything, …

They made me step back more.

What I Was Actually Looking For

I wasn't looking for perfection.

I wasn't looking for everything to be fixed overnight.

I was looking for something I could feel.

Something I could trust.

Something that didn't shift
every time things got hard.

I was looking for:

Consistency
Calm
Space to be myself
Someone who could handle my emotions
without becoming overwhelmed by them

I was looking for
someone who felt steady.

What Drew Me Back

I came back
to the parent who stayed steady.

Not perfect.

But steady.

The one who:

Didn't react to every emotion
Didn't take everything personally
Didn't give up when things felt distant

The one who:

Stayed calm when I was unsure
Listened when I didn't have the right words
Gave space without disappearing.

The one who didn't try to control the outcome…

but stayed present through the process.

What That Felt Like

With that parent…

I didn't feel pressure.

I didn't feel like I had to perform.

I didn't feel like I had to explain everything perfectly.

I didn't feel like I had to choose sides.

I felt:

Safe
Seen
Allowed to grow
Allowed to come back in my own time

And that changed everything.

What Most People Don't Realize

Children don't come back
because they are told to.

They come back
because something feels different.

They come back to:

Peace over pressure
Consistency over intensity
Presence over control

They come back
to what feels steady.

What I Wish Parents Understood

I didn't need perfection.

I didn't need you to fix everything.

I didn't need the right words every time.

I needed you to stay.

To stay steady
when I didn't know what I felt

To stay calm
when I was unsure

To stay present
even when I pulled away

That is what I came back to.

What This Means for Parents

If you are a parent reading this…

This matters more than anything else:

You don't have to be perfect.

You don't have to fix everything.

You don't have to say everything right.

You have to be steady.

Steady in your tone.
Steady in your presence.
Steady in your love.

Even when:
They pull away
They don't respond
They seem distant

Because what feels steady…

becomes what feels safe.

And what feels safe…

is what they return to.

What This Means for Adult Children

If you are the child—now grown—reading this…

You didn't come back by accident.

You came back
to what your heart recognized
as steady and safe.

And if you haven't come back yet…

That doesn't mean it's over.

Sometimes it just means
you haven't experienced
what feels steady yet.

What This Changes About the Story

This is not about:

Who was better
Who was right
Who did more

This is about:

What felt safe
What felt consistent
What allowed connection
to grow again

Faith and Restoration

There is something deeply important here.

God is steady.

He does not shift
based on our emotions.

He does not pull away
when we struggle.

He remains.

Scripture tells us:

"Jesus Christ is the same yesterday and today and forever."
— Hebrews 13:8

That is what draws us to Him.

His steadiness.

His consistency.

His unchanging presence.

And when we reflect even a part of that…

we become a place
others can return to.

What Healing Looks Like

Healing doesn't always begin
with both people at the same time.

Sometimes it begins
with one person choosing to stay steady.

One person choosing:

Not to react out of fear
Not to withdraw out of hurt
Not to control out of insecurity

But to remain.

To be present.

To be consistent.

And over time…

That becomes the place
others feel safe returning to.

Closing Thought

I didn't come back
because everything was perfect.

I came back
because something felt steady
when everything else felt uncertain.

Closing Line

Children don't return to pressure.

They return to peace.

What I Understand Now

CHAPTER 9

What I Understand About Both of You Now

I didn't understand it then.
I didn't have the words to explain what I was feeling.
But what I understand now is something very different.

A Moment I Couldn't Avoid Anymore

I used to see things
in parts.

One side.
Then the other.

I didn't understand
what each of you carried
individually.

I only knew
how it felt to be in the middle.

I didn't expect it to happen like that.

It wasn't planned.
It wasn't a deep conversation.
It was a normal moment—
the kind that usually passes without meaning anything.

We were sitting across from each other.
Not as parent and child anymore…
but not fully as two adults either.

There was a pause.

And for the first time,
I didn't feel like I had to protect myself.

I just asked.

"Did you think I didn't want you?"

They didn't answer right away.

Not because they didn't hear me…
but because something in them shifted.

And in that moment,
I saw something I had never seen before.

Not distance.
Not disinterest.

Pain.

The kind that had been there
the whole time—
just hidden in ways I didn't understand as a child.

And that was the moment everything began to change.

Through the Eyes of the Adult I Am Now

There was a time
when everything felt divided.

Two homes.
Two experiences.
Two different feelings
that didn't always make sense together.

One felt easier.
One felt harder.

One felt steady.
One felt uncertain.

And without realizing it…

I started to form conclusions.

Not just about what I experienced…

but about what it meant.

What That Looked Like in Real Life

It looked like comparing things
without even trying to.

Noticing:

How one house felt
compared to the other

How conversations went
in one place versus another

How I felt
when I walked in
and when I left

It looked like:

Relaxing more in one place
and being more aware in another

Feeling understood in one moment
and misunderstood in another

And slowly…

those experiences became beliefs.

What I Thought Then

I thought:

One parent understood me.
The other didn't.

One parent showed up.
The other didn't.

One parent felt safe.
The other didn't.

And from those thoughts…

I built a story.

A simple one.

One was right.
One was wrong.

It made things easier to understand.

But it wasn't the full truth.

The Weight I Didn't Know I Was Carrying

There was something else underneath that story.

The feeling that I had to choose.

Not always out loud.

But inside.

Who feels easier?
Who do I go to?
Who understands me more?

And even when I didn't want to choose…

it felt like I already had.

What That Did Inside of Me

It created tension.

Because loving one
started to feel like
I was hurting the other.

Understanding one
started to feel like
I was being disloyal to the other.

And even when no one said it directly…

I felt it.

That pressure to choose
doesn't always come from words.

Sometimes…

it comes from the situation itself.

What I Understand Now

Now I see something
I couldn't see before.

It wasn't that one loved me

and the other didn't.

They both loved me.

But they loved me
through different abilities.

Different experiences
Different strengths.
Different struggles.

What That Means

One may have had the ability
to stay calm and steady.

The other may have been overwhelmed
and unsure how to respond.

One may have known
how to create safety.

The other may have wanted to…

but didn't know how.

What This Changes

This changes everything.

Because now the story is not:

One loved me.
One didn't.

The story becomes:

They both loved me.

But they showed it differently.

What I See About Both of You Now

I see things I missed before.

I see:

Effort
in ways I didn't recognize

Pain

in ways I didn't understand

Fear
in ways that looked like distance

I see that neither of you were perfect.

But neither of you were without love.

What I No Longer Need to Do

I no longer need to compare.

I no longer need to choose.

I no longer need to carry
what was never mine to hold.

I can see both of you
for who you are.

Not perfect.

Not the same.

Although both important
in my story.

What This Means for Healing

Healing doesn't come
from choosing one over the other.

It comes from understanding both.

Understanding:

Why one felt easier
Why one felt harder
Why I responded the way I did

And allowing all of that
to exist…

without needing to divide it.

What This Means for Parents

If you are a parent reading this…

Your child does not need

to choose between you.

They need the freedom
to love both of you
without feeling disloyal.

When a child feels safe
to love both parents…

they begin to feel whole again.

What This Means for You

If you are the child—now grown—reading this…

You are allowed to:

Understand both
Feel compassion for both
Acknowledge what was hard
Recognize what was good

Without losing yourself
in the process.

What I Wish I Could Say Now

If I could say something clearly…

it would be this:

"I didn't stop loving either of you."

"I was trying to understand something
that felt divided inside me."

"And now…

I see more than I did before."

Faith and Restoration

God does not ask us
to choose between people
in order to heal.

He invites us to see clearly.

To understand deeply.

To release what we carried
that was never ours.

Scripture reminds us:

"Be kind and compassionate to one another, forgiving each other…"
— Ephesians 4:32

Compassion grows
when understanding replaces assumption.

And forgiveness begins
when the full story is seen.

What Healing Looks Like

Healing looks like this:

"I see both of you now."

Not through the eyes of confusion.

But through the eyes of understanding.

Closing Thought

You were never meant
to carry a divided heart.

Closing Line

Healing begins
when you no longer have to choose
who to love.

CHAPTER 10

Letting Go of What I Carried

I didn't understand it then.
I didn't have the words to explain what I was feeling.
But what I understand now is something very different.

Through the Eyes of the Adult I Am Now

I held onto things
I didn't know how to release.

Feelings.
Beliefs.
Moments that stayed longer
than they should have.

I thought holding on
would help me understand.

But it didn't.

Now,
I understand what it means
to let go.

There were things I carried
for a long time…

So long
that I didn't even realize
they were heavy.

They became normal.

They became part of how I thought…
how I responded…

how I saw myself.

And because I carried them quietly…

no one knew they were there.

Sometimes…

not even me.

What That Looked Like in Real Life

It didn't look like something obvious.

It looked like patterns.

It looked like:

Overthinking everything I said
Replaying conversations in my mind
Wondering if I had done something wrong

It looked like:

Trying to keep people happy
Avoiding anything that could create tension
Taking responsibility for things
that weren't mine

It looked like:

Feeling uneasy when things were calm
Expecting something to change
Preparing for something to go wrong

It looked like:

Trying to fix things
before they even broke

And I didn't always know why.

What I Was Carrying

I was carrying beliefs
I formed when I was younger.

Beliefs like:

"I have to get this right."

"I need to keep things peaceful."
"If something goes wrong… it might be me."

I was carrying:

Guilt
Responsibility
Fear
Confusion

All tied to something
I believed as a child.

What I Understand Now

Not everything I carried
was mine.

Some of it came from misunderstanding.

Some of it came from silence.

Some of it came from trying to make sense
of something I wasn't meant
to understand alone.

And some of it…

was never mine to carry
in the first place.

How It Followed Me

What I carried
didn't stay in childhood.

It followed me
into adulthood.

Into relationships.
Into decisions.
Into how I saw myself.

It showed up as:

Trying to please everyone
Struggling to set boundaries
Feeling responsible for how others feel
Avoiding conflict at all costs

It showed up as:

Fear of losing people
Fear of getting it wrong
Fear of not being enough

All connected to something
I believed long ago.

The Moment Things Began to Change

Things didn't change all at once.

They changed
when I started asking a simple question:

"Is this mine?"

And for the first time…

I allowed myself
to answer honestly.

What I Began to See

I began to see that:

I was not the reason
I was not too much
I was not the problem

I was someone
who had been carrying
what didn't belong to me.

What Letting Go Really Means

Letting go
is not pretending it didn't hurt.

It's not minimizing the past.

It's not ignoring what was real.

Letting go is choosing:

"I don't need to carry this belief anymore."
"I don't need to hold this responsibility anymore."

It's releasing

what no longer belongs to you.

What I Had to Release

I had to release:

The belief that I caused it
The belief that I wasn't enough
The belief that I needed to fix everything

I had to release
the responsibility
I placed on myself
as a child.

What Happened When I Let Go

When I began to let go…

Something shifted.

Not all at once.

Not perfectly.

But slowly.

I felt lighter.

I felt clearer.

I felt less responsible
for things that were never mine.

And in that space…

Something new began to grow.

Peace

What This Means for You

If you are carrying something
that has followed you for years…

Pause here.

Ask yourself:

"Is this mine?"

If it isn't…

you are allowed
to let it go.

What This Means for Parents

If you are a parent reading this…

Your child may be carrying things
you never meant for them to carry.

And unless it is spoken clearly…

they may continue carrying it
into adulthood.

Sometimes healing begins
with simple words:

"That was never yours to hold."

Faith and Restoration

God does not ask us
to carry what He already carried for us.

Scripture reminds us:

"Come to Me, all who are weary and burdened, and I will give you rest."
— Matthew 11:28

That includes the weight
you picked up as a child.

Restoration includes release.

Letting go
is part of healing.

What Healing Looks Like

Healing looks like this:

"I don't need to carry that anymore."

Not because it didn't matter…

But because it was never mine
to begin with.

Closing Thought

You can keep carrying
what no longer belongs to you…

or you can choose
to release it.

Closing Line

Healing begins
when you put down
what you were never meant to carry.

What This Means Now

If you are the parent:
There may be things your child carried
that you never saw.

Not because you didn't care—
but because they didn't know how to show you.

If you are the child—now grown:
What you carried was real.
The weight…
the questions…
the meanings you formed.

But you are allowed to release
what no longer belongs to you.

If you are both:
Letting go is not about forgetting.
It is about no longer holding onto a version of the story
that keeps you stuck in the past.

And sometimes…
healing begins
when we stop carrying what was never ours to hold alone.

PART 3 — Restoration

CHAPTER 11

Choosing to Forgive What I Now Understand

I didn't understand it then.
I didn't have the words to explain what I was feeling.
But what I understand now is something very different.

Through the Eyes of the Adult I Am Now

For a long time,
forgiveness felt complicated.

It felt like letting something go
that still mattered.

It felt like saying
something was okay
when it didn't feel okay.

But I see it differently now.

And that changes everything.

There was a time
when forgiveness felt impossible.

Not because I didn't want peace.

But because I didn't understand
what had actually happened.

It's hard to forgive
when something still feels confusing.

It's hard to let go
when something still feels personal.

For a long time…

I held onto what I felt.

Not always with anger.

But with questions.

Questions that didn't have answers.

Questions like:

"Why did it feel like that?"
"Why didn't things stay steady?"
"Why did it seem like they pulled away?"

And without answers…

it was hard to release anything.

What That Looked Like in Real Life

It looked like remembering moments
that still didn't make sense.

Replaying conversations
and trying to understand them differently.

Feeling something in my chest
when certain memories came up…

even years later.

It looked like:

Wanting to move forward
but feeling pulled back

Wanting peace
but not knowing how to get there

It looked like:

Saying, "I'm fine" …
but knowing something was still unresolved

What I Thought Forgiveness Was

For a long time…

I thought forgiveness meant:

Saying it didn't hurt
Pretending it didn't matter
Acting like everything was okay

I thought forgiveness meant
I had to ignore what I felt.

So, I didn't move toward it.

Because what I felt was real.

What Changed Everything

Forgiveness didn't begin
when I forced myself to let go.

It began
when I started to understand.

When I saw:

They didn't reject me…
they struggled

They didn't stop loving me…
they didn't know how to stay steady

They didn't choose distance…
they didn't know how to close it

And when I saw that…

something shifted.

What Understanding Did

Understanding didn't erase the pain.

But it changed
what the pain meant.

It took something personal…

and gave it context.

And when something has context…

it becomes easier
to release.

What Forgiveness Really Is

Forgiveness is not saying:

"It didn't matter."

Forgiveness is saying:

"I understand more now…
and I'm choosing not to carry this the same way anymore."

It's not excusing behavior.

It's releasing the weight
that came from misunderstanding it.

What Made Forgiveness Possible

I didn't arrive at forgiveness
because everything was perfect.

I arrived at forgiveness
because I saw the full picture.

I saw:

The love that was there
The strength that was missing
The fear that got in the way
The confusion that created distance

And once I saw all of that…

holding onto blame
no longer felt like healing.

How Repair Makes Forgiveness Possible

Forgiveness doesn't happen
in isolation.

It grows
where something has been acknowledged.

Where something has been seen.

Where something has been repaired.

Not perfectly.

But honestly.

Repair says:
"That mattered."
"That affected you."
"I see it now."

And when something is seen…

it becomes easier to release.

Because forgiveness is not built
on pretending it didn't hurt.

It is built
on knowing it mattered.

What Forgiveness Is Not

It is not:

Forgetting
Agreeing
Allowing unhealthy patterns to continue

Forgiveness does not remove boundaries.

It removes the weight
of what you were carrying inside.

What Forgiveness Does

Forgiveness creates space.

Space for peace
Space for clarity
Space for growth
Space for healthier connection

And sometimes…
space to move forward
even if everything
is not fully restored.

What This Means for You

If you are not ready to forgive…

That's okay.

Forgiveness cannot be forced.

It grows from understanding.

And if you've been walking through this…

understanding is already beginning.

What This Means for Parents

If you are a parent reading this…

There may be things your child is still holding.

Not because they want distance…

but because they haven't fully understood yet.

Your role is not to demand forgiveness.

Your role is to:

Stay steady
Stay open
Stay willing

And allow healing
to happen over time.

What I Realize Now

Forgiveness didn't change the past.

But it changed me.

It changed how I carried it.

and how I saw it.

And it gave me something
I didn't have before.

Freedom.

Faith and Restoration

Forgiveness is at the center
of God's heart.

Not as pressure…

but as freedom.

Scripture tells us:

“Be kind and compassionate to one another, forgiving each other, just as in Christ God forgave you.”
— Ephesians 4:32

God does not force forgiveness.

He invites us into it.

Because He knows something
we often don’t realize at first:

Forgiveness doesn’t just free the other person.

It frees you.

What Healing Looks Like Now

Healing looks like this:

“I understand more now.”

“And because I understand…
I am choosing to release
what I carried.”

Not all at once.

Not perfectly.

But honestly.

Closing Thought

Forgiveness didn’t begin
when everything made sense.

It began
when I allowed myself
to see the full story.

Closing Line

Understanding opens the door…

Forgiveness is the step
that sets you free.

What I Understand Now

PART 4 — Moving Forward

CHAPTER 12

What We Can Build From Here

I didn't understand it then.
I didn't have the words to explain what I was feeling.
But what I understand now is something very different.

Through the Eyes of the Adult I Am Now

There was a time
when I thought everything
was already decided.

That what had happened
defined what would always be.

But I understand now…

there is still something ahead.

And it doesn't have to look
like what was behind us.

There was a time
when everything felt like it had already happened.

Like the story was already written.

Like what was broken
would always feel broken.

Like what was lost
could not be rebuilt.

But I see something different now.

The story is not finished.

What I Understand Now

What happened mattered.

What I felt was real.

What was confusing
what was painful
what didn't make sense

All of it mattered.

But it doesn't have to define
what comes next.

What That Means

The past explains things.

But it doesn't have to control everything.

It gives context.

But it doesn't have to decide
what we build moving forward.

What I No Longer Need

I no longer need:

Everything to be perfect
Everything to be explained
Everything to feel the way I wish it had

Because I understand something now.

Growth doesn't come from going backward.

It comes from building forward.

What We Can Build Now

We can build something different.

Not based on:

What went wrong
What was missing
What didn't happen

But based on:

What we understand now
What we are willing to do differently
What we are learning

What That Looks Like in Real Life

It looks like:

Slower conversations
More listening
Less reacting

It looks like:

Asking instead of assuming
Pausing instead of pushing
Staying present instead of pulling away

It looks like:

Allowing space for growth
instead of expecting perfection

What This Requires

It requires something simple.

But not always easy.

Awareness.

Awareness of:

How we respond
How we affect each other
What we bring into thc rclationship

Because when we become aware…

we begin to change.

What This Means for Parents

If you are a parent reading this…

You have more influence than you realize.

Not by controlling outcomes.

But by creating an environment
that feels:

Steady
Safe
Open

Your child does not need perfection.

They need consistency.

They need to know:

You are still here
You are still willing
You are still learning

What This Means for Adult Children

If you are the child—now grown—reading this…

You are not the same person you were then.

You understand more now.

You see more clearly.

And that gives you something powerful:

Choice.

You can choose:

How you respond
What you carry
What you release
What you build

What We Can Do Differently Now

We can:

Listen without preparing a response
Speak without trying to control the outcome
Stay present when things feel uncomfortable

We can:

Allow conversations to be imperfect
Allow growth to take time

Allow relationships to rebuild slowly

What Rebuilding Actually Looks Like

Rebuilding is not one big moment.

It's small moments.

Moments like:

A calm conversation
A genuine apology
A willingness to listen
A decision to stay

I remind myself to repeat this over time.

That is what builds trust again.

What I Understand About Time

Time does not heal everything.

But what we do with time…

does.

If nothing changes…

time just passes.

But if we grow…

if we learn…

if we choose differently…

Time becomes part of healing.

What This Means for Relationships

Relationships are not rebuilt
by forcing closeness.

They are rebuilt
by creating safety.

By showing up consistently.

By allowing space.

By choosing connection
without pressure.

Faith and Restoration

There is something deeper here.

God is not finished with our stories.

Even when things feel broken…

He restores.

Scripture reminds us:

"And I will restore to you the years that the locust has eaten…"
— Joel 2:25

Restoration doesn't mean
everything goes back to the way it was.

It means something new
can be built from what we understand now.

Something stronger.

Something clearer.

Something rooted in truth.

What Healing Looks Like Moving Forward

Healing looks like this:

"I understand more now."

"And I'm choosing to build differently."

Not perfectly.

But intentionally.

What We Carry Forward

We don't carry the confusion.

We don't carry the blame.

We don't carry the weight

that was never ours.

We carry:

Understanding
Awareness
Growth
Grace

Closing Thought

The past may have shaped part of your story.

But it does not have the final word.

Final Line

What we build from here
can be stronger
than what was behind us.

PART 4 — Moving Forward

CHAPTER 13

What We Never Said to Each Other

I didn't understand it then.
I didn't have the words to explain what I was feeling.
But what I understand now is something very different.

Through the Eyes of the Adult I Am Now

There were things
that stayed unspoken.

Not because they didn't matter…
but because we didn't know
how to say them.

And over time,
silence filled in the gaps.

But silence
doesn't always tell the truth.

There are things
that were always there…

But were never said.

Not because they didn't matter.
Not because they weren't felt.

But because
no one knew how to say them
without making things worse.

So instead…

they stayed quiet.

And in that silence…
we started to believe things
that were never actually true.

What I Never Said as a Child

I didn't say:

"I miss you when I'm not with you."

Because I didn't know
if that would hurt someone else.

I didn't say:

"I feel different in each place."

Because I didn't have the words
to explain what that meant.

I didn't say:

"I don't understand what's happening."

Because I thought
I was supposed to already know.

I didn't say:

"I need help."

Because I didn't know
how to ask for it.

What I Was Feeling Instead

I was feeling:

Confused
Overwhelmed
Pulled in two directions
Unsure of where I belonged

Trying to understand
something that felt bigger than me.

But what came out…

didn't sound like that.

It sounded like:

"I don't want to go."
"I'm staying here."
"I don't like it there."

And those words…

changed things.

What You May Have Heard

You may have heard:

"They don't want me."
"They are choosing someone else."
"I'm losing my child."

And that hurt.

More than I understood at the time.

Because I didn't see
what those words touched in you.

I only knew
what I was feeling inside me.

What You May Have Never Said

You may not have said:

"I don't know what to do right now."

"I'm afraid of losing you."

"I don't know how to fix this."

"I don't want to make this worse."

You may not have said:

"I'm trying…
but I don't know if it's working."

So instead…

you adjusted.

You pulled back.
You paused.
You became careful.

And to me…

that felt like distance.

The Space Where We Missed Each Other

There was a space
between what I felt
and what you heard.

Between what you felt
and what I saw.

And in that space…

we missed each other.

Not because love wasn't there.

But because
understanding wasn't.

What I Wish We Could Have Said

I wish I could have said:

"I don't want to choose between you."

"I don't understand why this feels hard."

"I still love you
even when I don't know how to show it."

And maybe…

you would have said:

"I'm not giving up on you."

"I just don't know how to reach you yet."

"I love you
even when this feels uncertain."

What Changes Now

Now…

I see something I didn't see before.

We were both feeling something real.

We were both trying
in ways we didn't know how to explain.

We were both affected
by something neither of us
fully understood.

And what we didn't say…

became the story we believed.

The Truth That Was Always The

The truth is:

I didn't stop loving you.
You didn't stop loving me.

We just didn't know
how to say what mattered most
when it mattered most.

What Can Be Said Now

But here's what matters now.

It's not too late
to say what wasn't said.

It's not too late
to understand what was missed.

It's not too late
to replace silence
with clarity.

What Does This Means Moving Forward

We don't have to stay
in what was misunderstood.

We can begin again
with what we know now.

We can say:

"That wasn't rejection."
"That wasn't the full story."
"That wasn't the end."

A Different Kind of Conversation

The conversation now
doesn't have to be perfect.

It just has to be honest.

Slower.
Softer.
More understanding
than before.

Because now…

we are not speaking
from confusion.

We are speaking
from clarity.

Closing Thought

Not everything that was felt
was ever said.

But that doesn't mean
it's gone.

Closing Line

Sometimes healing begins
not with new words…

but with finally understanding
the ones that were never spoken.

What I Understand Now

Letter 1

What I Couldn't Say Then (Child → Parent)

Focus: Emotional Expression Without Words
Purpose: To give voice to feelings that were not understood in childhood.
Outcome: Builds understanding that behavior was not rejection, but confusion.

I want to say something
I didn't know how to say before.

Not because it wasn't there…

But because I didn't understand it yet.

There were moments
when I felt confused.

Moments when I pulled away.
Moments when I didn't have the words
to explain what I was feeling.

And I know now…

that what I said
and how I said it
may have felt like rejection to you.

But I need you to hear this clearly.

I never stopped loving you.

Even in the moments
when I didn't know how to show it.

Even in the moments

when I didn't know how to stay connected.

I was trying to understand something
that felt bigger than me.

I didn't know how to explain
why things felt different.

I didn't know how to say
what I needed.

So, what came out…

wasn't always clear.

Looking back now…

I can see more than I did before.

I can see that you were trying.

I can see that you didn't always know
what to do.

I can see that there were moments
you felt unsure…
maybe even afraid
of losing me.

And I didn't see that then.

I only saw what I felt.

But now…

I understand more.

I understand that love was there.

Even when it didn't always feel steady.

I understand that what I thought was distance
may have been uncertainty.

And I understand
that we were both trying
in ways we didn't know how to explain.

There are still things
that were hard.

Things that mattered.

Things that affected me.

And I'm not pretending
those things didn't exist.

But I am choosing
to see them differently now.

Not through confusion.

But through understanding.

And because I understand more…

I'm choosing something else too.

I'm choosing to release
what I carried for so long.

Not because it didn't matter.

But because I don't need
to carry it anymore.

I don't need to carry
the belief that I wasn't enough.

I don't need to carry
the responsibility I placed on myself.

I don't need to carry
what was never mine.

What I want now
is something simple.

Not perfect.

Just real.

A relationship
that can grow from here.

One that is:

Honest
Steady
Open

Willing

I don't expect everything
to be fixed overnight.

But I am open
to building something new.

And I want you to know this…

I see you differently now.

Not perfect.

Not as someone who got everything right.

But as someone who loved me
and didn't always know how to show it.

And that changes everything.

I'm here.

And I'm willing
to move forward
together.

Letter 2

What I Didn't Understand Then (Parent → Child)

Focus: Parental Insight and Reflection
Purpose: To acknowledge moments of misunderstanding and emotional disconnect.
Outcome: Reduces defensiveness and increases empathy.

There are things
I wish I had said sooner.

Things I didn't always know

how to put into words.

Not because I didn't feel them…

But because I didn't always know
how to express them in the moment.

There were times
when I felt like I was losing you.

Times when I didn't understand
what you were feeling
or how to reach you.

And in those moments…

I didn't always respond the way I wish I had.

Sometimes I tried too hard.

Sometimes I pulled back.

Sometimes I didn't know
what to say at all.

But I need you to hear this clearly.

I never stopped loving you.

Not for a moment.

Even when I didn't know how to show it in a way you could feel.

Even when things felt distant.

Even when I didn't know how to connect.

My love for you
never changed.

There were times
when I felt unsure.

Unsure of what to say.
Unsure of what to do.
Unsure of how to fix
what felt like it was breaking.

And instead of handling those moments
with strength…

I sometimes responded
with hesitation.

Or silence.

Or distance.

Not because I didn't care.

But because I didn't know
how to move forward
without making things worse.

And I see now…

how that may have felt to you.

I see now
that what I thought was protecting the situation…

may have felt like I was pulling away.

And for that…

I am sorry.

Not from a place of guilt.

But from a place of understanding.

I see more now
than I did then.

I see how important
consistency is.

I see how much
emotional safety matters.

I see how my responses
affected what you felt.

And I want you to know…

I am still learning.

Still growing.

Still willing.

You didn't need me to be perfect.

But you did need me
to be steady.

And I understand that now.

If I could go back…

I would do some things differently.

I would have listened more.

I would pause more.

I would stay calmer.

But I cannot change the past.

What I can do…

I can be present now.

And build something different
moving forward.

I don't expect everything
to be easy.

But I am willing
to keep showing up.

To keep learning.

To keep growing.

To create something
that feels safe…

not just said.

I am here.

And I am not going anywhere.

What once felt like rejection
may have only been love
that didn't yet know how to stay steady.

And now… you can see it differently.

And now… you understand more.

You see what was hidden.
You see what was never said.
You see what was always there.

And because of that—
you don't have to carry the same story anymore.

You can choose peace.
You can choose understanding.
You can choose to build something different from here.

Because what was once misunderstood
is no longer the end of the story…
it is the beginning of healing.

- -

Letter 3

When I Didn't Feel Safe (Child → Parent)

Focus: Emotional Safety Awareness
Purpose: To help parents understand how children experience emotional environments.
Outcome: Increased awareness of tone, reactions, and consistency.

There were things I felt
that I didn't know how to explain.

Not because they weren't real…
But because I didn't understand them myself.

There were moments
when something inside me didn't feel steady.

Moments when I didn't know
what I was walking into.
Moments when I didn't know
how things were going to feel.

And I didn't have the words to say,
"I don't feel safe."

So instead…
I said things like,
"I don't want to go."

But what I meant was something different.

I meant,
"I don't know how to relax."
"I don't know what to expect."
"I don't know how to explain what I'm feeling."

And I know now…
that may have sounded like rejection to you.

But it wasn't rejection.

It was a feeling
I didn't yet understand.

Looking back…
I can see more clearly now.

I can see that love was there.
But I didn't always feel steady enough to receive it.

And that difference…
mattered more than I realized.

I'm not saying this to blame.

I'm saying this
so you can understand
what I didn't know how to say before.

Because now…
I do.

And now…
we have a chance
to build something
that feels not only loving…

but safe.

Letter 4

Learning to Create Safety (Parent → Child)

Focus: Building Emotional Safety
Purpose: To help parents recognize the importance of steady, calm responses.
Outcome: Development of safer, more predictable interactions.

There is something I understand now
that I didn't understand then.

That love alone
is not always enough
if it doesn't feel safe.

I loved you.

That never changed.

But I can see now
that there may have been moments
when you didn't feel steady with me.

Moments when my tone,
my reactions,

or my emotions
may have felt overwhelming.

And I didn't see that then.

I thought love would be enough.

But now I understand…

It wasn't just about what I felt.
It was about what you experienced.

And if there were times
when you didn't feel calm,
didn't feel safe to speak,
or didn't know how I would respond…

I can see how that would have affected you.

I wish I had understood that sooner.

Not so I could be perfect…

But so I could have been more steady.

I am learning now
that safety is built in how we respond,
not just in what we say.

And I want to grow in that.

Not just for myself…

But for you.

So that moving forward,
what you feel
matches what I've always meant:

Love
that is steady
and safe.

Letter 5

What I Carried That Wasn't Mine (Child → Parent)

Focus: Releasing False Responsibility
Purpose: To help the child release guilt and self-blame.
Outcome: Improved self-worth and emotional relief.

There is something I carried
for a long time.

Something I didn't talk about.

Because I thought
it was mine to carry.

I thought
I was part of the reason
things changed.

I thought
if I had been different…
quieter…
easier…

maybe things would have stayed the same.

No one told me that directly.

But as a child…
I filled in the blanks.

And I carried that belief
longer than I realized.

But I understand something now

that changes everything.

It was never mine to carry.

I was a child
trying to understand something
that was bigger than me.

I wasn't the reason.

I was responding
to what I didn't understand.

And I need you to know…

If I ever seemed distant,
confused,
or unsure…

It wasn't because I didn't care.

It was because I was trying
to make sense of something
I didn't have the tools for yet.

And now…
I'm letting that weight go.

Not because it didn't matter.

But because it was never mine.

Letter 6

When I Didn't Know What to Do (Parent → Child)

Focus: Parental Vulnerability and Growth
Purpose: To acknowledge uncertainty without assigning blame.
Outcome: Builds trust through honesty and humility.

There were moments
when I didn't know what to do.

Moments when I could feel
that something wasn't right…
but I didn't know how to fix it.

And in those moments…
I didn't always respond with clarity.

Sometimes I reacted.
Sometimes I hesitated.
Sometimes I pulled back.

Not because I didn't care.

But because I didn't know
how to move forward
without making things worse.

I can see now
how that may have felt to you.

Like distance.
Like disconnection.
Like I wasn't showing up.

But the truth is…

I was there.

I just didn't know how to reach you
in the way you needed.

And I wish I had known.

I wish I had slowed down more.
Listened more.
Stayed steadier.

But I understand now…

And that understanding
changes how I move forward.

I may not be able to change
what happened then.

But I can choose
how I show up now.

And I choose
to keep learning
how to reach you
in a way that feels real.

Letter 7

Choosing to Move Forward (Child → Parent)

Focus: Healing and Forward Movement
Purpose: To shift from past hurt toward future relationship building.
Outcome: Encourages openness and willingness to reconnect.

There are things
that were hard.

Things that mattered.
Things that stayed with me.

And I'm not pretending
those things didn't exist.

But I am choosing
to see them differently now.

Not through confusion…
but through understanding.

I can see now
that there was more happening
than I realized at the time.

I can see
that we were both feeling something…

but neither of us
knew how to say it clearly.

And because I understand more now…

I'm choosing something else.

I'm choosing
not to stay in what hurt.

I'm choosing
not to carry what I no longer need.

I'm choosing
to move forward.

Not perfectly.

Not all at once.

But intentionally.

I don't expect everything
to be fixed overnight.

But I am open
to building something real.

Something honest.
Something steady.
Something different.

And that matters to me.

Letter 8

Commitment to Show Up Differently (Parent → Child)

Focus: Consistency and Repair
Purpose: To establish ongoing commitment to growth and connection.
Outcome: Builds trust through consistent effort and presence.

There is something I want you to know
as we move forward.

I am still here.

Not just in words…
but in willingness.

Willing to listen.
Willing to pause.
Willing to understand.

I know now
that showing up
is more than being present.

It is how I respond.
How I listen.
How I stay steady
even when things feel hard.

I may not get everything right.

But I am committed
to coming back.

To repairing when needed.
To growing where I need to grow.
To creating something
that feels safe for you.

I don't expect perfection
from you.

And I don't expect it from myself.

But I do believe
we can build something meaningful
from where we are now.

Step by step.

Moment by moment.

Together.

Letter 9
My Letter to You

What We Carry Forward

There was a time
when everything felt unclear.

What I felt…
What you felt…
What it all meant…

It didn't always make sense.

And when something doesn't make sense…
we fill in the gaps.

Sometimes with fear.
Sometimes with assumption.
Sometimes with stories
that stay with us longer than we realize.

But now…
there is something different.

There is understanding.

Not perfect understanding.
Not complete answers.

But enough to begin seeing clearly.

Enough to begin letting go
of what was never fully true.

What I Know Now

I know that love
was not always missing.

Sometimes it was quiet.
Sometimes it was uncertain.
Sometimes it didn't know
how to stay steady.

But it was there.

I know that what felt like rejection
was not always rejection.

Sometimes it was confusion.
Sometimes it was fear.
Sometimes it was not knowing
what to do next.

What This Changes

When the meaning changes…
everything begins to shift.

Not because the past disappears.
But because it no longer holds

the same weight.

We are no longer carrying
the same story.

What We Carry Forward

We don't carry the blame.
We don't carry the confusion.
We don't carry the weight
that was never ours.

We carry:

Understanding
Awareness
Grace
And the ability
to choose differently now

What Is Still Possible

Not every relationship
restores the same way.

Not every conversation
happens all at once.

But something is always possible:

Clarity
Growth
Peace
And sometimes…
reconnection

What Matters Most

It does not take perfection
to begin again.

It takes willingness.

Willingness to see differently
Willingness to understand more deeply
Willingness to stay
when it would be easier to pull away

Closing Thought

You are not where you were.

You understand more now.
You see more clearly now.

And that changes
what comes next.

Final Line

What once felt like the end…
may have only been
the part of the story
you hadn't yet understood.

What I Understand Now

Workbook & Reflection Section

Understanding, Healing, and Moving Forward

How to Use This Section

You do not need to complete everything at once.

Take your time.

Some questions may feel easy.
Some may take longer to answer.

Be honest.
Be patient with yourself.
There is no "right" answer.

This is not about being perfect.

It is about understanding
what you experienced
and how it shaped you.

UNDERSTANDING YOUR EXPERIENCE

Reflection 1 — What Did I Believe?

Think back to your childhood experiences.

What did you believe was happening at the time?

What did you believe about your parent(s)?

What did you believe in yourself?

What did you think certain moments meant?

□ Write your thoughts.

Reflection 2 — What Did It Feel Like?

Not what happened…

but what it felt like.

When did you feel most confused?

When did you feel most at peace?

When did you feel unsure or unsettled?

□ Write your thoughts.

WHAT I UNDERSTAND NOW

Reflection 3 — What Do I See Differently?

After reading this book.

What do you understand now that you didn't before?

What has changed about how you see your parent(s)?

What has changed about how you see yourself?

□ Write your thoughts.

Reflection 4 — Separating Truth from Belief

Complete these statements.

What I thought was true...

What I understand now...

What I believed about myself...

What I know now...

□ Write your thoughts.

WHAT I CARRIED

Reflection 5 — What Have I Been Carrying?

Be honest here.

What responsibility did I take on that wasn't mine?

What emotions have I carried for years?

What patterns do I notice in my life now?

□ Write your thoughts.

Reflection 6 — Is This Mine to Carry?

Ask yourself:

Is this belief still true?

Did this responsibility belong to me?

Do I still need to carry this?

□ Write your thoughts.

Reflection 7 — What Can I Release?

You do not have to carry everything forward.

What belief can I let go of?

What responsibility can I release?

What do I no longer need to hold?

□ Write your thoughts.

Reflection 8 — What Do I Want Instead?

If you release something…

you make space for something new.

What do I want to feel instead?

What do I want my relationships to look like?

What kind of person do I want to become?

□ Write your thoughts.

Reflection 9 — What Can I Do Differently Now?

Growth is not about the past.

It's about what you do next.

How can I respond differently in relationships?

What boundaries do I need to set?

How can I create emotional safety?

□ Write your thoughts.

Reflection 10 — What Am I Building Now?

You are not stuck in your past.

You are building your future.

What kind of relationships do I want to build?

What do I want to be known for?

What values matter to me now?

□ Write your thoughts.

Reflection 11 —Restoration

Take a moment to reflect.

What has God shown me through this journey?

What do I need to release to Him?

What am I trusting Him to restore?

□ Write your thoughts.

Reflection 12 —Encouragement

You are not who you were then.

You understand more now.
You see more clearly.
You are growing.

What you experienced matters.

But it does not define
what you can become.

□ Write your thoughts.

Books by Dr Janet Olivares

Finding Self with God
Day by Day

Forgive
Let Go for Real

Hooked and Confused
Understanding Porn, Pressure and Identity in a Digital World

Love Never Left
When Marriage Feels Lost God Restores

Parenting Teens
Steady Parenting Even When the Kids Push Away

Suicide
Hope beyond a Moment

Two Houses One lonely Heart
Divorce through the Eyes of a Ten Year Old

What I Understand Now
It's the Love I Couldn't See Healing the Distance Between Parents and Adult Children.

To order books from Amazon directly

To order books wholesale from Extended Distribution Amazon

To contact Rapha Center:
559-478-6077
www.raphaccc.org
info@raphaccc.org

Dr. Janet Olivares

Dr. Janet Olivares, Ph.D., is a clinician certified in Marriage and Family Therapy, Crisis and Abuse Therapy, Domestic Violence and Intervention Therapy, and Substance Abuse and Addiction Therapy with a strong commitment to restoring individuals and families impacted by trauma, separation, and divorce. Her work centers on promoting healing, healthy relationships, and family reunification through compassionate, evidence-informed care.

Dr. Olivares is especially passionate about supporting children and parents navigating the emotional challenges of co-parenting and family transitions. She brings awareness to the long-term impact of relational trauma and advocates approaches that foster stability, communication, and resilience within families.

In addition to her clinical work, Dr. Olivares is an accomplished author. Through her writing, she integrates clinical insight with accessible guidance to support individuals and families facing complex emotional and relational challenges.

Dr. Olivares remains dedicated to empowering others through education, advocacy, and a holistic approach to healing that honors both emotional and relational well-being.

What I
Understand Now
Its the love I couldn't see healing the distance
between parents and adult children
DR. JANET OLIVARES

PARENTING EDUCATION CERTIFICATE OF COMPLETION

This certifies that ______________________
Participant Name has successfully completed the parenting education program based on:

What I Understand Now — It's the love I couldn't see healing the distance between and parents and adult children

The participant has completed assigned reading, reflection exercises, and participation requirements designed to support healthy parent-child relationships, emotional regulation, and constructive discipline practices.

Program Provider / Organization:

____

Instructor / Facilitator:

____

Total Instruction Hours: ____________________
Date Completed: _____________

Location (City/State):

____

Facilitator Signature: ______________________________
Date: _____________

Printed Name & Title: ___________________________________

Contact Information: ____________________________________

Acceptance of this certificate is subject to the discretion of the referring court or agency

www.ingramcontent.com/pod-product-compliance
Lightning Source LLC
LaVergne TN
LVHW010620100826
845148LV00014B/3050

* 9 7 8 1 6 0 7 8 9 3 8 4 4 *